ZOOKEEPERS

P9-DEW-464

eXtreme jobs

Big Buddy BOOKS
Extreme Jobs

Sarah Tieck

ABDO
Publishing Company

VISIT US AT
www.abdopublishing.com

Published by ABDO Publishing Company, 8000 West 78th Street, Edina, Minnesota 55439.

Copyright © 2012 by Abdo Consulting Group, Inc. International copyrights reserved in all countries. No part of this book may be reproduced in any form without written permission from the publisher. Big Buddy Books™ is a trademark and logo of ABDO Publishing Company.

Printed in the United States of America, North Mankato, Minnesota.
062011
092011

 PRINTED ON RECYCLED PAPER

Coordinating Series Editor: Rochelle Baltzer
Contributing Editors: Megan M. Gunderson, BreAnn Rumsch, Marcia Zappa
Graphic Design: Marcia Zappa
Cover Photograph: *Photolibrary*: Jochen Tack/Imagebroker.net.
Interior Photographs/Illustrations: *AP Photo*: Topeka Capital-Journal, Ann Marie Bush (p. 21), The News Tribune, Russ Carmack (p. 21), Discovery Networks U.S. (p. 17), Salina Journal/Tom Dorsey (p. 5), Danny Lawson/PA Wire URN:6722472 (Press Association via AP Images) (p. 15), The Evansville Courier & Press/Erin McCracken (p. 13), Petar Petrov (p. 19), Giovanni Rufino/NBC NewsWire via AP Images (p. 27), Marcio Jose Sanchez (p. 29), Mary Schwalm (pp. 13, 15), David Zalubowski (p. 15); *Getty Images*: Claire Greenway (p. 9); *Photolibrary*: Lineair (pp. 7, 23), Mauritius (p. 27), The Print Collector (p. 25), Olaf Schubert/Imagebroker.net (p. 11), Jochen Tack/Imagebroker.net (p. 23); *Shutterstock*: Rebecca Abell (p. 30), Michelle D. Milliman (p. 30), Monkey Business Images (p. 30).

Library of Congress Cataloging-in-Publication Data

Tieck, Sarah, 1976-
  Zookeepers / Sarah Tieck.
     p. cm. -- (Extreme jobs)
  ISBN 978-1-61783-029-7
  1. Zoo keepers--Juvenile literature. I. Title.
  QL50.5.T54 2012
  636.088'9--dc23
                                 2011018118

CONTENTS

ZOOKEEPING 101

Interesting animals live all over the world. Some of them live in zoos or animal parks. Workers called zookeepers take care of them. They also help people learn about them.

Zookeepers keep these animals safe and healthy. They may feed tigers or file an elephant's nails. Now that's an extreme job!

Zookeepers must be extra careful around big or dangerous animals.

A DAY AT WORK

Zookeepers have a very active job. They walk or stand for most of the day. Each zookeeper cares for different animals.

One of the first things zookeepers do each day is feed the animals. Some animals eat grasses, fresh fruits, or vegetables. Others eat meat or fish.

Zookeepers make sure each animal gets the food it needs. For example, giraffes eat leaves and hay.

7

Animals at zoos live in **exhibit** areas. These often look natural. But, they are man-made. So, workers must keep the water and land in each exhibit clean and safe.

Zookeepers spend part of their day cleaning exhibits. They pick up poop and leftover food. They wash surfaces with water and special soap. And sometimes, they give animals baths. This can be a gross, dirty job!

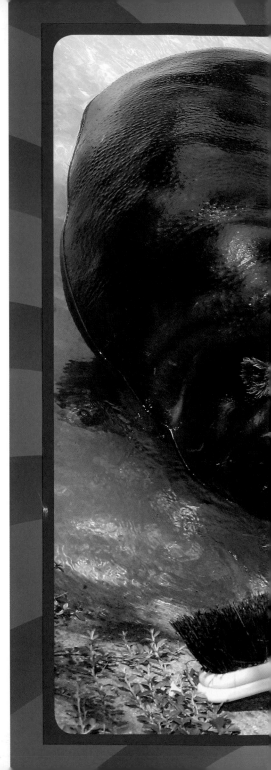

In the wild, pygmy hippos chew foods that keep their teeth healthy. In zoos, they eat differently. So, zookeepers help keep their teeth clean by brushing them.

WILD LIFE

As zookeepers feed animals and clean **exhibits**, they observe each animal. They make sure the animals are not hurt or sick. Animals often hide signs they are sick. In the wild, this keeps them from looking weak. But in zoos, zookeepers pick up on these signs. For example, animals may stop eating.

Animals can spread diseases to people. And, people can also make animals sick. So, zookeepers must be careful when working closely with animals.

Zookeepers make sure animals get enough play and exercise. They may give them games or toys for play. Sometimes, zookeepers hide food for the animals to find. Such activities help the animals stay active.

GEARING UP

Zookeeping is a tough job! People can get sick from touching animals. So, zookeepers wash their hands often. They may work outside in hot or cold weather. So, they wear sunblock, hats, and clothes that cover their skin.

Zookeepers use many tools to do their job. They use rakes, shovels, brushes, and hoses for cleaning. They use measuring tools to measure each animal's food.

Besides cleaning, zookeepers use hoses to help cool animals on hot days.

Zookeepers may wear masks so they don't share sicknesses with the animals.

Zookeepers often carry paper and pens to write notes about animals.

TRAINING ANIMALS

Zoo animals are not pets. They are wild animals. They may bite, scratch, or kick. Still, zookeepers work close to them.

Zookeepers sometimes train the animals so they can work with them more safely. This also makes it easier for the animals to live in a zoo. For example, zookeepers train elephants to lift their feet. Then, zookeepers can file their nails.

Steve Irwin was a famous zookeeper and television star. In the 1990s, he became known as the Crocodile Hunter.

FACT ALERT

Jack Hanna is a famous zookeeper from the Columbus Zoo in Ohio. In the 1980s, he began appearing on television with animals. He enjoys teaching people about them.

ANIMAL HOSPITAL

Zookeepers make sure animals are healthy and eating well. When animals have babies, zookeepers may move them to a separate area. There, they can watch them closely and care for them if needed. Zookeepers may also give special care to very old, sick, and young animals.

Sometimes, young or sick animals need to be handfed.

Zookeepers take action if an animal is sick. They may bring it to an animal hospital. If an animal is very large, a **veterinarian** visits it instead. At most big zoos, such doctors are part of the staff.

Animals may need to wear casts or bandages. Zookeepers may apply and check these.

A sick animal may need to have an operation. Before this, a doctor gives it medicine that makes it fall asleep.

READY, SET, GO!

Zookeepers are specially trained. They know how to clean, feed, watch, and care for zoo animals. Most zookeepers have a college **degree** in a science. Many have studied animal science.

Gaining practice working with animals is important for people who want to be zookeepers. They do this by working in places such as **veterinarian** offices or farms. They may also help at zoos before they become zoo workers.

Zookeepers are experts about the animals they work with. Some work with just one type of animal. Others work with many different animals.

THEN TO NOW

Long ago, wealthy people such as kings kept unusual animals for fun. Workers cared for the animals. One of the first known animal collections was in Egypt in 3500 BC. It included hippos, elephants, and wildcats.

Many early zoos were called menageries (muh-NAJ-rees). These were often small. And, only certain people were allowed to visit.

Over time, public zoos were established. At first, zoo animals were kept in cages. In time, people made bigger homes for them.

Today, many **exhibits** look like animal homes in the wild. When making living spaces, zoo workers consider each animal's needs. They want them to live well at the zoo.

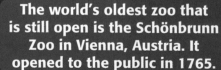

The world's oldest zoo that is still open is the Schönbrunn Zoo in Vienna, Austria. It opened to the public in 1765.

Natural-looking exhibits may have rocks, plants, and water.

FACT ALERT

The first zoo in the United States opened in 1874 in Philadelphia, Pennsylvania.

BEHIND THE SCENES

Zookeepers don't always work directly with animals. They also keep notes and records about animals. And, they teach visitors about zoos and the animals in them.

Zookeeping can be hard, dirty work. But, it helps provide fun and education for visitors. And, a zookeeper's extreme job keeps animals safe and healthy!

Zookeepers usually let mothers care for their young. But, they may work with young animals to train them as they grow.

WHEN I GROW UP...

Explore parts of a zookeeper's job now!

Zookeepers work in zoos around the world. Ask an adult to help you plan a visit to a nearby zoo.

Zookeepers feed animals and keep their spaces clean. If your family has a pet, you can learn how to take care of it. You can also practice by doing chores at home, such as cleaning your room.

Zookeepers use math to measure food and medicine properly. So, be sure to listen carefully in math class!

IMPORTANT WORDS

degree a title given by a college, university, or trade school to its students for completing their studies.

exhibit a public showing or display.

veterinarian (veh-tuh-ruh-NEHR-ee-uhn) a doctor who treats animals. A short name for veterinarian is "vet."

WEB SITES

To learn more about zookeepers, visit ABDO Publishing Company online. Web sites about zookeepers are featured on our Book Links page. These links are routinely monitored and updated to provide the most current information available.

www.abdopublishing.com

INDEX